This book belongs to:

Given with Love By:

The snow was softly falling
from the cold winter sky.

Yaya
Looked up with a twinkle in her eye.

I love you more than
all the snowflakes
that are flying so high!

Yaya
loves you more than
all the
marshmallows in
this hot cocoa mug!

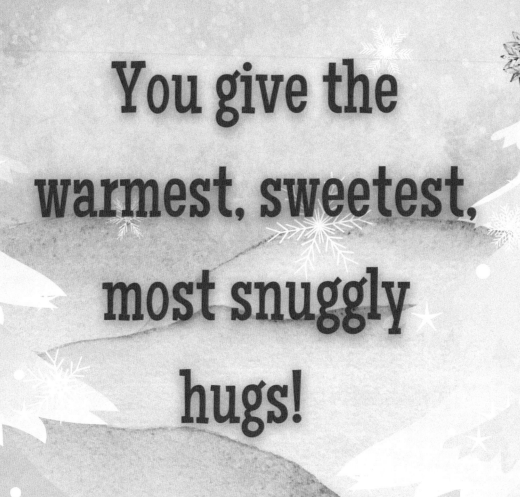

You give the warmest, sweetest, most snuggly hugs!

Yaya

loves you more than
all the bright
morning sun rays.

You bring me joy
every single day!

Yaya

loves you more than
all the twinkling
lights!

Your love can brighten even the darkest of nights.

Yaya
loves you more than
all the cozy winter
socks!

You make me smile
every time we talk.

No matter how many storms cross the cold winter sky.

Please always remember, that
Yaya
Loves You More

than all the snowflakes

that will fly!

Made in the USA
Middletown, DE
01 January 2025

68631672R00015